Gun Control for Polar Bears

Christopher Michael Carter

Supposed Crimes LLC • Matthews, North Carolina

This book is a work of fiction. Names, characters, places, and incidents are products of the author's imagination or are used fictitiously. Any resemblance to actual events or locales or persons, living or dead, is entirely coincidental.

All Rights Reserved
Copyright © 2016 Christopher Michael Carter

Published in the United States.

First Edition

ISBN: 978-1-938108-95-2

www.supposedcrimes.com

This book is typeset in Goudy Old Style, licensed by Ascender Corporation.

To my wife, for holding down the fort while I chase my dreams. Your love, support and encouragement knows no bounds and I am eternally grateful.

And to my family and friends for their patience and support, thank you so much.

This world is full of people who will want to detour you and tell you "No" but you learn that the only people that really matter to you are the ones who will give you a chance and tell you "Yes". Onward and upward; keep going and ignore the rejection. Embrace optimism and positivity; put your blinders on to the negativity in this world and reach your destination with pride.

Godspeed & God bless.
Christopher Michael Carter

Gun Control For Polar Bears

1.

Sky
I'd love to see the sky, but-
I'm afraid of heights
I'm tired of seeing the ground
I see it all too often
Crashing, burning, crashing
Always crashing
Will I ever reach a plateau
Taller than a mere hill?

2.

How much longer can this coalition of cannibals coexist
While everyone's starving?
Peeking at each neighbor
Wondering when they'll trip
And fall behind
Stragglers make the best lunch

Gun Control For Polar Bears

3.

Welcome to the edge of tomorrow
You've awoken 52 years old
And your babies are now parents
Welcome to next week
You've awoken 65 years old
Retired
You collect your check and hope for the best
Welcome to next year
You've awoken 68 years old
Yet another mandatory birthday card
From your grown children
And the children of children
Welcome to the day
You've awoken in a box that's barely bigger than the body
That use to encompass your soul
Everyone cries
But you understand
You have an agenda
And it's time

4.

A clearing found
A clearing in the conversation to mention her
An oasis
An oasis of silence to which she can mutter his name
Tears
Puddle, ponds, lakes, oceans apart
Two human beings are perfect for one another
But they're strangers
Nothing known about one another
No face, no voice, no touch
...How sad

5.

Happy meat eaters
Is all I see
All around me
I don't like that I indulge
And I'm not sure why
I don't like it
But I do it anyway
I wish I could say no
But it's all smiles
The fork harpoons the meat
As if I'm Captain Ahab finally catching up with my old foe
The knife saws through the flesh, vigorously
The blood shown
I like it rare
My nicotine, my caffeine
My vice
She's red
She's the reason I can't let it all go
How can something so wrong
Taste so right?
And so Ahab enjoys his prize
Happy meat eaters
Am I in denial?

6.

Racial struggles have reemerged
   Still
   Racism isn't the issue it used to be
But it still boggles my mind to find racists
Especially in this day and age
But I hope, pray, and predict
That the percentage of racism and bigotry
Will plummet drastically in the next ten years
Out with the old
In with the new
Once we get the old mentality out of sight
We'll be a lot better off as a society
There will always be fighting and bickering
But it doesn't have to be over petty things
It's time to usher in new
Leaders, treaties, loves, friendships, inspirations, & goals
And it's time to toss out old
Traditions, rules, barriers, mindsets, hidden agendas, & wars
Out with the old & in with the new

7.

Love
Is love attention?
Is love affection?
Is it in a touch?
Is it in a voice?
A sound frequency?
A picture? A pixel?
Is love the question or the answer?
Is love a statement or a reply?
Can it be described or captured in text?
If not, why is there a written word for it?
Is love in a gift?
Is it a gift?
Is love only found in joy?
And joy in love?
What is it to love ~
And to be in love?
Is love caring?
Is love sparing?
What is it to be in love with other emotions?

8.

What is the coal that fuels us?
The match that sparks our anger
We're a large locomotive with millions of cars
That love to derail
The heat, the passion
Fuels such a train
Be it hate, anger, both
It pushes, it chugs
A destination reached
But we've lost more than a few cars

9.

He calls for his father
The one never there
Left at birth, he had only a mother
He doesn't mind
It's life
A life his father didn't want
And so with a mother's love he grew to be something
Something his predecessor couldn't be
...Dad

10.

They gave birth to a beautiful baby girl
And named her-
Dammit, where have you been? There are dishes to be done!
So her life took on her namesake
Dish after dish
Disappointing her parents after each one
If only she was born with hands
Do you think they'd be disappointed then?

11.

I'm bitter
I'm lost, I'm cold
I just want out
Is that so wrong?
I'm broken
I'm bruised, I'm swollen
I just want my medicine
Is that so wrong?

12.

I wish I could hear
What dogs are thinking
Why they do what they do
What they really think of us
I wish I could feel
Dog's emotions
When they feel what they do
I wish I could sense
What dogs sense
How they know danger, fear
I wish I could
See how they see
Smell how they smell
Taste how they taste
I wish I could
Elect
A dog for president
A canine would have
Better judgment than most politicians
Groundbreaking!
It would be the first
Time
A politician would be referred to as
Man's Best Friend

Gun Control For Polar Bears

13.

Hands on a face
Hands on a clock
Always spinning
360
Round & round
Always making you look around
Eyes chasing
The arrows pointing every which way
Keeping the mind busy
Always on your toes
The face
Of the clock, however
Always staring directly at you
It watches you
While you're concerned with where its hands guide you
It watches your every move
It examines you
While you chase the arrows round
Entertained
Like a child
It's a babysitter
A passive babysitter

14.

Some of us
People
Humans
Are allergic to many things
Mold
Cats
Dogs
Plants
Medicines
Fabrics
Materials
But allergies make me wonder
Are animals allergic to anything?
Are plants?
And...
Specifically
Are plants and/or animals allergic to us?
Could we
Humans
Perhaps
Be an allergy?

15.

Anger
The mirror's broken
The shards sit in the sink
Some reflect her and her surroundings
Some reflect what might have been
Some wait to be used
Revenge
The drawer's open
The knives sit amongst one another
Some reflect the kitchen light
Some reflect what might be
But the right one waits to be used
Vengeance
Is hers

16.

He lifts the stone
To prove his strength
The crowd's in awe
The girls cheer
His parents gush with pride
The mayor's hand is prepared for shaking
Lights flash
The camera's eye winks
The press readying release
The paper's about to go to print
His muscles strain
His bones crack
His knees buckle
Then it happens...
His legs break beneath him
The stone falls
His body
Along with all pride & hope
Broken
Everyone goes on about their day
Unfazed
Unscathed
Unlike the man
Lying before them
The man of inconsequence

17.

Kick the sand
Kick it hard, kick it far
Throw it up so you can see
It sparkle in the sun
Take the biggest handful of sand
You can
Throw it to the sun
And wait for a beautiful sculpture
To fall from the sky
If we truly are getting closer
To the sun
Eventually
The beach will be glass
And will be as reflective
And as beautiful
As the water that surrounds it

18.

The moon glows
The sun shines
The night carries
The day drags
The villagers wait
Wait for twilight

19.

He pulls into the driveway
Headlights off
He can smell it in the air
He saw it before he hit the door
Before he turned the doorknob
He knew what she was doing
Every day before he came home
He knew it
He knew what she was doing
The doorknob's turned
He could smell it in the air
Entering the house
Sure enough
Just as he suspected
Dinner was ready
A feast to behold
As it is every night
She was making him love her
More and more
Every day and every night

20.

The star fell that night
The campers saw
They wished
And so they caught every fish
There was to catch
The deer wished
And so the hunters lost their ammo
The bears saw it too
They also wished
And so the campers went to sleep
And left the coolers of fresh fish
Unattended

21.

No papers will be printed
No footage will be seen
No scriptures will be found
No remnants of a memory
Of God's secret creatures
No photos will be taken
No letters will be written
No sights will be sketched
No thought, no recollection
Of God's secret creatures
No words will be whispered
And no names will be mentioned
No dreams will be dreamt
And no signs will be on the radar
Of God's secret creatures

22.

Flowers
They feel
It's painful to be picked
Some find it excruciating
Others see it as their lives
Awaiting to be
The one to be
Picked next

23.

The lights flicker
We saw them running
But couldn't catch up to them
Down the hall
They scaled the walls
But we couldn't catch up to them
They cried for help
But kept running
When will the shadows stop
And when will we catch them?

24.

A cookie is just a cookie
No more
No less
But a child will risk
Life & limb
To find out what kind
Is kept inside
That cookie jar

25.

Casting the stone
Shattering the church
Faith fallen
Broken at the alter
The candles
The statues
Melt under pressure
Cherubs weep
A new church
A new stone is cast

26.

From pen to paper
My heart to yours
A love through ink
I hope you feel
The emotion
Put into such a quill
The tear stains
Around
Each sentence
Could show you
How I feel

27.

Life is a rollercoaster
Full of ups & downs
Plenty of curves, swerves, & twists
Life is a rollercoaster
Be the maintenance man
Make sure, yourself
That it doesn't derail

28.

He's weird
She's strange
They're in love
How normal

29.

The town's people grab their oars
The oars hung up only
To be
Used
This once a year
The annual liquid parade
The children
And elderly
In their life vests
With smiles to boot
The same follows...
For the people in the suburbs
And the cities
And everyone rejoices and
Celebrates
The liquid parade

30.

They crawl
They slither
They find a way
They scour
They scale
They find their way
They seek
They seed
They're here

31.

The feet
They walk
The feet
They stalk
The feet
They wear
...
They wither
Alas
The feet
They rest

32.

She sweats
She grunts
Screams, cries, screams, swears
A labor of love
A labor of lust
She pushes
The crying
She hears the crying
A new face is born
And the face is hers
She sweats
She sighs
Cries, laughs, cries, thanks
She breathes

33.

He was a captain
A captain
Without a ship
He wandered through
The desert
For ten long years
Surviving on cacti
Random desert life
And an oasis
That became his home
No man is an island
But this man at least
Had his own
The island in the middle
Of the world
The island
In the middle of nowhere
But like everything else
The oasis dried up
His home dried up
Captain's been walking
Walking, walking
For many years
He bears many cactus scars
Covered
He's skin, bones
And organs
Literally
He's fading away
Like grains of sand
That blow away in the night
You'll never see
The same grain twice
Just like you'll
Never
See the captain twice
Not this captain

Not this man
The man who sailed
The sea
Of sands
Some say you can still spot him
The Cactus Captain of the Desert
But you'll never see him twice

34.

Snakes and stones
May try to take my throne
But words
Will never turn me

35.

Lawyers
Generals
Senators
Random animals
Waiters
Activists
Priests
Random animals
Hunters
Salesmen
Dancers
Random animals
Snipers
Teachers
Writers
Random animals
Artists
Athletes
Presidents
Random animals

36.

You've poisoned me
You've
Infected me
You've planted
A seed
In my heart
Somehow
You've seduced me
And now
I'm yours

37.

A memorial
An obituary
For my valentine
She loved
She was loved
She was survived
By a gallery
Of hearts
So I stand today
For a memorial
An obituary
For my valentine

38.

I am the night
I am the shadows
And in the absence
Of light
You'll find me
Waiting
For you

39.

For as long as she remembered
She hadn't had a home
Like an outcast
A stray cat
She wandered town to town
Like a drifter
Occasionally she found a place
Abandoned
And she would make it her home
At least for a little while
And this house was no different
No one was home
It appeared
Smelled a little
But she could deal with that
Flies & gnats
Cover its insides
Its furniture, its walls
She could hear them buzzing
Before even turning on the lights
And that's when she saw
The bodies
Two recliners, two bodies
One woman
One man
Perhaps
Husband & wife
She thought
TV trays still in their laps
Occupied by maggots
And a slit in each throat
From one ear to the next
She just stood there
Staring
That's all she could do

Spiders crawled from the mouths
And wounds
Of this couple
She didn't normally get squeamish
But this was a different occasion
She passed them
On into the kitchen
Everything seemed to be covered with a different bug
And that's when she heard
The whimper
She opened the pantry door
To find a little girl
She'd been crying
For so long her eyes were completely red
It dawns on her
What had happened
"Were they your parents?"
The little girl nodded wiping her face
The girl's just like her
A stray, a drifter
An orphan
"C'mon, kid," She said
Extending her hand to the child
"Let's go home...
Wherever that happens to be."
And so the two were odd
They shed their skin
As orphans and outcasts
And begin anew
As family

40.

The woman sits back on the couch
Her date on his knees before her
All he can hear is her moaning
The wind chimes outside
And the air conditioner
Though all muffled by her thighs
A nice ending
To a nice evening
None the less

41.

He arrived
He played
And no one paid
Until that night
When the world slept
He opened his dressing room
Door
To find
Tulips
All of them
And so he was paid
In tulips
Tulips for the Dream Cellist

42.

White t-shirts & black gloves
Is all he could see
The woman, they wore
White t-shirts & black gloves
White panties
And black knee-high platforms
They were all around him
Where has his course
Taken him?
Where has his ship
Landed?
They won't leave him
They surround him
"It's time to take the male back with us!"
One screamed
And so they did
The women of this
Odd planet
Brought the man back
In a bamboo cage
Where he was to be
Sacrificed
By their Queen
And with the women
She couldn't be happier

43.

The man's precision
Is fine tuned
He gets the envelope
In the mail
This man seeks
You out
And you
Are in his sights
This man
Is the gun

44.

You feel alone
Why?
Is it because it seems
Like no one cares?
Because mom & dad
Didn't think you were
Good enough?
Or because your friends
Didn't show up to your
Birthday party?
Or simply because you haven't come to accept
The fact
That you're dead

45.

The information leak
Downloading a possible future
Every key typed
Gets you closer to then
You will know more than you would without
You will carry more information
Than your neighbor
And faster & more precise at that
All hail
The information leak

46.

Life is time
Time is life
Time is money, time to spend
A life to spend
Remember; time is watching
Make it good

47.

The gravity
In my apartment sucks
The water from my air conditioner
Leaks up
Causing water stains
Upon my ceiling

48.

The man who laughs
The man who cries
The man who bares
The man who dies
The man who trips
The man who lies
The man who watched the world burn

49.

The chemicals
The same chemicals that form
You & I
Are the same chemicals
That form us
And would we have it
Any other way?

50.

Space
Why such a distance from man?
We climb the, literally, star studded ladder
To the black sky above
Space
Several times a year
Just to get a glimpse
Our ships sail through the anti-gravity sea
Always in search of
Space
Space for sale, space to claim

51.

She took a hit of acid
Not too long ago
The carpet began to crawl
It spread up the walls
Reaching the ceiling
Encompassing everything with carpet
Furniture, clothes, appliances, everything
Every move, every step, was one in rug burn
The carpet grew taller
Then the knock at the door
If she could find it
It was him
The neighbor from across the hall
He's returned her lawn mower
Just in time

52.

The space between
Science & laughter
The space between
Kisses & hugs
The space between
You & her
And her & him
Will never be the same again

53.

Freedom of speech
Freedom of heat in winter
Freedom of all the things
We choose to avoid
Freedom praised
Freedom ignored
Freedom chosen
Freedom struggled
Freedom fought
And ultimately
Freedom won

54.

People will die
It's sad but true
We all will die
Eventually
But with that said
It's time to kick
The pessimistic heathens of society
Aside
And live life
The way we were meant to
Within our time span
Before we meet our expiration date
We, the people
Are like milk
We can do a lot of good
Before it's our time to go

55.

The gates of hell open
And the demons escape
But for a day
   Just a day
To join in on the festivities
Cake & punch, cake & punch
Everyone enjoys the day out
And goes back in the box
When the party's over

56.

Evil wears pants
And the pocket
The pocket holds the killing hand
Yes, the killer has pockets
And the pocket
The pocket holds the killing hand
Evil deals the cards
And the pocket
The pocket beneath the table
Holds the killing hand
Now in the killer's hand

57.

It's Halloween
And the challenge was issued
The boy stepped up
Trick or treaters beware
For tonight the game begins
One point = five pieces of candy
He knows the score
He knows the neighborhood
And all the jack-o-lanterns in town
Should have been carved into teary frowns
For he is the Pumpkin Slayer

58.

It seems to be a general consensus
That racism is worse than homophobic bigotry
That the words "Nigger" & "Spic"
Are somehow worse than the words "Fag" & "Dyke"
Granted, these are all harsh words
But
While racism holds its gruesome
And harsh pastime in America
People of different ethnicities can
Now
These days
Vote, lead, & wed
But also in these days
In such a free country
We have trouble accepting different sexual orientations
Sure it can be glamorized on TV
But in seldom states
Can they wed
A simple thing such as marriage
Can't even be granted by the better portion
Of such 'free' states

59.

Ten toes
Feet are his business
His life, his thing
His fetish
He searches the boardwalk
Camera & binoculars onboard
The man gets photos of prospects
In his dark room
Deep in the bowels of his London apartment
He picks & chooses
His next victim
And continues his collection

60.

The burning
Damn the burning
Could someone spare
A glass of water
For this burning soul?

61.

He looks to the sky
She looks to the ground
They look good together
But they'll never see

62.

The walls look on
The floor walks on
The doors open
And
The air breathes on

63.

Politicians & whores
Politicians & whores
Onlookers in the streets
Watch dogs beware
Politicians & whores

64.

Skeletons
Skulls by the tons
Skeletime to pay
The piper once more
Skull by skull
Until payments no more

65.

Grass is green
Money is green
Oil is black
Oil is money
Blood is red
Flag stripes are red
Soldier blood is money

66.

The television is on
The minds are set
To record
The radio is on
The minds are
Tuned in
You now have the attention
The floor
Is yours

67.

The world is a racecar
It goes around
Fast
Fuel is burned
And a pit stop
Has been needed
For some time

68.

Flesh against flesh
Blood against blood
A marriage
Muscle & bone
Mind & body
Search long
Search deep
Take the reins

69.

The mailman is armed
Girl scouts are packing
The bag boy at the local grocery has a pipe bomb at home
The school janitor has a knife in his boot
The librarian has pepper spray on her desk
Bank tellers have their finger on the trigger beneath the counter
The bouncer has brass knuckles
The babysitter is strapping
And the coach has a night stick
Though we've tried
We're still a violent nation
And though we've come a long way
The paranoid state in which we were raised in
Has left us a nation of arms
And not a nation of rational thought
It's not that we're concerned about protection
We're concerned about the thought
Entertaining the mere idea that something could happen
Fear
Artificial fear

70.

The clouds are many
The sun is one
The souls are many
The God is one
The people are many
Society
Is one

71.

Children are abused everyday
What are they learning from it?
Children and adults alike
Are abusing everyday
What do you think they're learning from it?

72.

They left the movies
About a quarter to seven
They never left their sight
They never made it home

73.

Varicose stateliness
Alcohol mainlines
A mailbox in the middle of the ocean
Liver dining spots
Blood orange clots
A mailbox in the middle of the ocean
And the postman's at a stalemate

74.

Another child diagnosed
They have the cure
And we know it
But there's more money
In treatments & vaccines
Than in cures
And so
Another child dies slowly
While families pay for treatments
That everyone, doctors & parents alike
Knows won't make a difference

75.

Some say
   9-11 was a violent smokescreen
Drug dealers
Fuel dealers
One in the same
Everyone loves each other
While everyone is paranoid
Pearl Harbor was our link
To be heroes in the war
The World Trade Center gave us a link
To get at the oil fields
Keep everyone afraid of terrorists
While the black gold is stolen
   The youth are killed
   Running into battle
   The suits are rich
   Running to the banks
With thousands dead
How much is oil worth in blood?
   Others say the war following
   That dark morning
   Was nothing more than revenge
   Not about fuel or freedom
   But blood for blood
   What is the truth?
The truth is ugly
But everyone covers it up with drywall
   And patriotic wallpaper

76.

She was a dancer
Always on her feet
Until the day
She was stranded in the desert
And with no food
Her feet were first
To go

77.

The piano played
No one heard
No one saw
No one touched
But the piano played

78.

Her doll's hair rustled in the wind
Out by the swing set
Where she used to play
She would never go anywhere
Without the doll
Where did she go?
What could have happened
To that little girl?
And so the doll sits
And waits
For its friend to return

79.

Her teeth are the gates
To which
Behind are her breathy
Whispers contained
Should I pry them open
For a spell
My ears
Would be eternally grateful

80.

The man is loneliness
He takes the train
To get off at a town
Unknown to him
To a random bar
Where no one
Is aware of his existence
Much like home
This man is loneliness

81.

The villagers, they dance
In front of the fire
So their shadows tell stories
To their children & their shadows
The fire as their light
Their bodies as writing utensils
Every night they dance
Life is tradition
Tradition is life

82.

The leaves turn colors
As we all grey
The trees become bare
As we all die
The trees come back full
And strong
How will we come back?

83.

The blood on the arrow
Was cold
He hasn't been there
For hours
Alas
She's in love

84.

My eyes blur
As I write love letters
My eyes shut
As I write good night
I love you so much
I'm so happy I have you
To dream about

85.

It's night again
We've waited
We've slept
The slumber of the shamed
We've done our time
And it's night again

86.

She's guilty
I arrest her
And take her
To my love precinct
For caressing questions
And sensual interrogations
She'll cave, she'll be mine
My prisoner

87.

The ground opened up
The music blared
The earth had cracked
But no one cared
The sky rained down
Very little decayed
The world dried up
But no one stayed

88.

Burnt clouds hover
Over head
Larva filled dreamboats below
Our feet
With our brothers & sisters
At our sides
In a sea of biochemical
Warfare
A wave of opportunity builds
Behind us

89.

Halos
Pitchforks
Badges
Paperwork
A day in the life
Of God's double agent

90.

Notes on an accordion
    The comedian joked
Were like that of a heart
The more you squeeze
The more you get out
...Nobody laughed

91.

Her tears ignite
And the flames
Trickle
Upwards
From the letter she's read
When the flame hits her eyes
She sees the intentions behind the ink
As true

92.

I'm sleepy & sneezy but not a dwarf
I'm actually quite tall
I can be bashful & dopey
And even quite a doc
But I'm actually quite tall
Sometimes I can be grumpy
Because I am too tall
But I'd say generally I am happy
Happy with it all

93.

Native Americans
Jews
Christians
Blacks
Women
Gays
So forth and so forth
Throughout history
The discrimination list
Needs to end
Before we do

Gun Control For Polar Bears

94.

The picture's black
With silver bullets
Falling down
The picture's black
With voice over
On cue
This heart is
Pouring out
To the darkness
The gun is empty

95.

She walks
She continues to walk
The end is in the distance
The end is joy
The end is happiness
The road is littered
With sharp stones
Regardless of the pain
She treks on
The journey is hard
And littered with heartache
But the love at the end
Is healing
And the time spent in the curing joy
Will erase the aching road
Behind

96.

I'm content
I'm happy
I haven't said that
In so long
I'm not trying to escape
I'm home
I haven't said that
Ever

97.

We are all memory hoarders
Theory packrats
We hold on to so much
Often too much
Some
Get pitched
While some
Go in the yard sale
But we all have those
That we tuck away
The closets are full
The shelves in the garage are covered in dust
The storage shed is locked
We are all memory hoarders

98.

Enjoy the past
It is what it was
And was what it is
Push through the present
It's here regardless
And there's only one way through it
Brace for the future
It is coming
It is what it will be
And there's only
One way
Through it
Keep pushing

99.

The shadows
Wall walkers
Without the light
The shadows would not be
But too much light
And they would cease to exist
They crawl across the floor
They climb the walls and ceilings
Though they spend their time hiding
When the light fades
They are no more

100.

There's a figure
In the doorway
There's a figure
In the window
The figure
Watches you
Watches your every move
Counts your breaths and awaits in time
The figure anticipates everything you do
It knows you
It knows you want to
You can't seem to get past it
The figure
Is you

101.

You're paranoid
You won't drink the water
You won't use your debit card
You won't shop online
You won't make a phone call
You bar the windows and set up barricades
To keep danger out
Are you sure you're not just imprisoning yourself?
You're content
Stationary in your bomb shelter of a life
You won't accept or adapt to any changes
You won't stray from your normal path
You watch from the sides but won't get in the game
Are you even allowing yourself to live?
You're terrified
You won't open your door all the way
You watch from your window constantly
Everything's a potential threat
You point your finger
And place everyone and everything into categories
Are you sure you're not just making yourself a target?
You're skeptical
You won't believe anyone
You won't listen to anyone
You never believe gossip, hype, or hearsay
You question everything
Except your own beliefs
Are you sure you let the right ones in?

About the Author

Christopher Michael Carter was born on May 3rd, 1984 in St. Louis, Missouri. While he grew up writing different styles, mediums, and genres, *Gun Control for Polar Bears* is his first publication. In 2013 he was diagnosed with Multiple Sclerosis and despite the daily struggle he continues to fight and write. Christopher currently resides in Bevier, Missouri with his wife, his daughter, and his dog.

www.ingramcontent.com/pod-product-compliance
Lightning Source LLC
Chambersburg PA
CBHW050506120526
44588CB00044B/1624